Aging Parents
and Options in Care

Aging Parents
and Options in Care

A Simple Handbook
Making the Best Decisions
For Loved Ones During Stressful Times

Hillary Abrams

iUniverse, Inc.
New York Bloomington Shanghai

Aging Parents and Options in Care
A Simple Handbook Making the Best Decisions
For Loved Ones During Stressful Times

iUniverse books may be ordered through booksellers or by contacting:

iUniverse
1663 Liberty Drive
Bloomington, IN 47403
www.iuniverse.com
1-800-Authors (1-800-288-4677)

Because of the dynamic nature of the Internet, any Web addresses or links contained in this book may have changed since publication and may no longer be valid.

The information, ideas, and suggestions in this book are not intended as a substitute for professional medical advice. Before following any suggestions contained in this book, you should consult your personal physician. Neither the author nor the publisher shall be liable or responsible for any loss or damage allegedly arising as a consequence of your use or application of any information or suggestions in this book.

FOR ADDITIONAL INFORMATION, CONTACT THE AUTHOR AT:
www.HillaryAbrams.com

Cover Photo By Cory Killorin

ISBN: 978-0-595-46686-3 (pbk)
ISBN: 978-0-595-90981-0 (ebk)

Printed in the United States of America

To all the families who wait … including my own.

CONTENTS

INTRODUCTION

Let's be realistic—most people wait until they are in crisis mode to react to the declining health of aging parents, spouses, or loved ones. My own family members say they will cross that bridge when they come to it. If you are one of the few people who plans for these things, you are way ahead of the game, especially if you're planning ahead for yourself.

My career in health care started in 1991 in the pharmaceutical industry. For many years, I was continuously educated and trained in various disease states affecting the aging population. I provided valuable information to medical professionals to help them make important decisions in treating the progression of declining health in their patients.

In 2002, I realized the importance of taking care of aging loved ones when I became a caregiver to my mother during a period of health issues. Because my sister and her family lived 3,000 miles away, I took a leave of absence from work to help my mother recover from several major surgeries. This experience motivated me to help others during similar, stressful times and resulted in my transition into eldercare.

Currently, I communicate daily with families who are completely exhausted from caring for aging or ill relatives. I hear and see the stress that accumulates with these adult caregivers. They are trying to take care of children, deal with the strain this may be putting on their marriage, and continue to work, all while caring for an aging loved one. With no time to themselves, adult caregivers allow quality of life to fall low on their priority lists.

Throughout this book, I have addressed the most common issues and concerns to help caregivers make the best possible choices during difficult times. With little time to sift through hundreds of pages of a book or to spend hours researching options on the Internet, caregivers may need a resource to help them make decisions quickly.

My intention is to help you in the process of choosing the best living arrangements for loved ones whether you live close by or in another city or state. Keep in mind that if one option doesn't work out, there are many others to choose from. This book is a place to start examining options.I hope you find this information useful in navigating the way for your aging parents or loved ones so they can have the best care possible. Following your instincts and using this book will help you make those decisions. My thoughts are with you!

CHAPTER 1

THE ASSESSMENT

Studies show that most seniors want to stay in their homes as they age. However, many find themselves alone and isolated as their spouses pass away, or their children move out of state or focus on taking care of their own children. Regardless of the situation, it is important to deal with the challenges of declining health as we all age. The first step is determining options in care and living arrangements for your loved ones is to assess their daily activities.

Assessing the overall situation will allow you to look at their strengths and weaknesses. Seeking professional help from their physician, a social worker, nurse, or case manager can help guide you in putting a plan into action. Receiving financial and legal guidance will help lead to the best decisions available.

Alice, 80, and Jim, 83, have been married for almost 60 years. They've lived in the same house for over half of that time and are hesitant about moving into any type of retirement community. In the past few years, their levels of daily activity have decreased due to mobility issues and chronic health conditions.

Alice tires easily when cooking meals and doing light chores around the house, even with a housekeeper coming in twice a week. She still drives, but only during the daylight, and Jim doesn't drive at all. Her debilitating arthritis and high blood pressure is treated with different medications throughout the day and evening.

Jim had a stroke last year causing him to use a walker. At that time, the family, with the help of Jim and Alice's physician, stepped in and told him that Alice would be doing all the driving. He wears hearing aids and is in early stages of Alzheimer's disease. Jim also has incontinence issues. Alice monitors Jim for fear of his falling while he's showering. On several occasions, she has had to call 911 or a neighbor to come help him off the floor, since she isn't able to lift him herself.

Mary, their youngest daughter, lives in the same city; however, her two siblings are out of state. She is married, has two children in college, and works full time, yet she insists on attending her parents' doctor's appointments with them. Mary's co-workers are getting somewhat frustrated. On several occasions, she has had to leave work suddenly due to various issues with her parents. Based on Mary's most recent observations of her Mom and Dad, she and her siblings are concerned about their parents' health and safety. They have discussed this with their parents and have agreed that, on the next doctor's appointment, Mary will address these issues.

They continue to reassure their parents that no one is trying to take their independence from them. On the contrary, everyone wants Alice and Jim to be safe. This is the time to explore all the possibilities before something serious happens, and they are making decisions from crisis mode.

To make any transitions as smooth as possible, take the following into account: Include the persons needing care in the decision-making process as much as possible. They will feel a sense of control over their lives. This also allows for a positive approach in the process. Although you may not be able to adhere to their wishes, this approach generally helps in coming to an agreeable plan.

Focus on the strengths of your loved ones and their independence. Then they won't feel like their control is slipping away from them. It also encourages everyone involved to consider the person as a whole human being and not as someone unable to function independently in any area of life.

The following provides helpful information in determining the best options available:

- Create an "Assessment Form and Checklist" as a resource for your loved ones' needs. Re-evaluate the assessment with a healthcare professional every 3–6 months and review changes.

- Prepare a list of medications to be updated as necessary.

- Fill out a "Financial Worksheet" to help determine which housing and lifestyle changes are affordable.

- Make copies of the "Evaluation of Adult Living Facilities Form" that is provided in this book. Make copies to keep track of who you've called and where you've visited.

Keep all of this information in a tabbed notebook along with any changes in your loved ones' behavior, whether physical, emotional, or mental, and the dates these changes took place.

It is often helpful to include relevant information such as:

- Phone numbers and addresses of doctors and their specialties.

- A copy of insurance cards, both front and back.

- Pharmacy addresses and phone numbers.

- Contact information for neighbors.

- Phone numbers and addresses, including e-mail, of legal and financial consultants.

- The security alarm company information and security code.

- Bank account information, including safe deposit boxes.

- Insurance policy information.

- Any other pertinent details you may need in case of an emergency.

When determining the type of care your loved ones need, consider the following points:

- Talk to your loved ones and ask their opinions.

- Consult with their physicians or a health care professional.

- Closely observe them while they are performing their daily activities.

- How safe are they in their home? Driving? Do they lock the door? Is the stove off? Do they use the ashtray?

- Has their personal hygiene or the level of cleanliness in the house changed?

- How are they walking? Do they avoid stairs?

- How is their eyesight? Hearing? Memory?

- How often do they leave the house? Do they have excuses about why they aren't leaving the house as much?

- Write down your concerns in order of most importance.

- What can your loved one afford? Can family members contribute?

- Can medical insurance or other benefits offer assistance?

Assessment Checklist

When determining the needs of your loved one, pay close attention to what they can and cannot do.

Personal Care:	Independent	Some Assist	Full Assist
Oral Hygiene			
Grooming			
Walking			
Bathing/Showering			
Meal Preparation			
Bathroom Use			
Eating			
Medication Reminders			

Housekeeping:	Independent	Some Assist	Full Assist
Laundry and Ironing			
Keeping Home Clean			
Making Beds			
Changing Linens			
Answering Phone and Door			

Caring for House Plants			
Taking Out Trash			
Caring for Pets			

Companionship:	Independent	Some Assist	Full Assist
Paying Bills			
Exercising			
Shopping			
Driving			
Doctor's Visits			
Social Activities			

Functional Limitations (Make notations as needed):

Bowel Control _____ Bladder Control _____ Hearing _____

Vision _____ Emotional Stability _____

Speech _____ Cognitive Ability _____

Medical Needs:	Independent	Some Assist	Full Assist
Taking Vital Signs			
Catheter Care			
Incontinence Care			
Range of Motion			
Skin Care			
Turning in Bed			
Eating			
Oxygen Therapy			
Wheelchair and Scooter Transfer			
Bed and Tub Transfer			
Lifts/Walkers			

The following is a list of supplies that may be needed. Review this list with a medical professional.

Medical Equipment and Supply Checklist:

Blood Pressure Cuff ___	Commodes ___	Diabetes Care ___
Foot Care ___	Gloves ___	Hot/Cold Therapy ___
IV Supplies ___	Incontinence Products ___	Lift Chairs/Belts ___
Mobility Products ___	Orthopedic Care ___	Security Necklace ___
Ostomy Products ___	Oxygen Supplies ___	Syringes & Disposals ___
Skin Care ___	Stockings ___	
Urology Supplies ___	Walkers/Walking Aids ___	
Wheelchair ___	Wound Care Products ___	

Alice had always kept her home spotless. Recently, Mary started noticing that when the housekeeper isn't there, her parent's bed is not being made. At times, dishes sit in the sink all day. The mail sits on the kitchen table in a pile. Mary wonders if the bills are getting paid on time. When she offers to help out with paying them, her father refuses assistance. He told her that he has always paid the bills himself and he always will. Mary sees bruises on her father's arms, but Jim says he doesn't know how he got them. There are times when he will not wear his hearing aids.

The front headlight of their car is cracked, and the rear bumper has a sizable dent that was not there a few weeks ago.

Mary is making notations in her assessment to review with their physician next week.

Almost half of older adults do not follow their medication regime properly, and this results in approximately one-third of hospitalizations due to mistakes and forgetfulness. With many elderly people taking multiple medications throughout the course of the day, it is imperative that they have a clear understanding of when they should take pills.

Labeling weekly pill cases and daily reminders may lessen any confusion. Keep track of medications and make necessary changes with this log sheet. Use this as a source to take on their medical appointments and review with a professional. A pharmacist or healthcare professional can advise you of potential drug interactions and possible side effects.

Medication Log Sheet

Medication/Dose AM	Mid-Day	PM	As Needed
1.			
2.			
3.			
4.			
5.			
6.			
7.			
8.			
9.			
10.			

Alice takes her blood pressure medications in the morning along with a cholesterol-lowering prescription. She takes arthritis medication twice a day, in the morning and evening, a pill for pain as needed, and a pill to help her sleep every night.

Jim takes almost all of his medications in the morning, including numerous cardiovascular medications and an Alzheimer's drug. He takes his incontinence medication in the evening and a pill to help him sleep every night. For two weeks, he must take an antibiotic for a urinary tract infection once a day in the morning.

Once a month, Mary fills color-coded pill cases for her parents, and their names are boldly printed on each case. This lessens the chances of her parents taking each other's pills. So far, Alice and Jim have been compliant in taking all their medications each day.

Financial Assessment Worksheet

Involve your loved ones by setting up a meeting with their accountant or financial advisor to discuss expenses, savings, and the assets of their estate. This worksheet will be a source for housing and lifestyle changes as everyone explores the options available. Use their checkbook register to calculate additional expenditures.

Household Income (Monthly)

Social Security _____

Employment Income _____

Retirement/Pension _____

Investment Income _____

Alimony _____

Other Income _____

Total Income _____

Assets (Current Market Value)

House/Condominium _____

Other Property _____

Stocks and Bonds _____

Pension (IRA, 401K) _____

Savings/Money Market Accounts _____

Certificates of Deposit _____

Insurance (Cash Value) _____

Annuities _____

Checking Account Balance _____

Automobile(s) _____

Prepaid Burial _____

Furnishings _____

Collectibles _____

Jewelry _____

Other _____

Total Assets _____

Household Expenses (Monthly)

Mortgage/Rent _____

Utilities _____

Food _____

Transportation _____

Clothing _____

Medications _____

Insurance Premiums _____

Entertainment _____

Credit Card Payments _____

Loan Payments _____

Taxes _____

Home Maintenance _____

Other Expenses _____

Total Expenses _____

Now, calculate monthly disposable income by subtracting total expenses from income:

_____ - _____ = _____
(Total Income)   (Total Expenses)   (Disposable Income)

Monthly disposable income is the amount that can be used to pay for additional services, such as personal care. When the disposable income is small, consider whether it's possible to sell any assets to pay for the service choice. If so, consider how long income from the sale of assets can support the choice that has been made.

For example, Alice and Jim's home is paid for. Many years ago, Jim bought long-term care insurance policies for him and his wife. Most people of their generation didn't have the knowledge and foresight to invest in these types of policies. Once Alice and Jim's accountant determines their financial situation, options in living arrangements and care can be considered.

Mary will help her parents by contacting their long-term care insurance company regarding coverage. She will ask questions such as: What are the requirements for the policy to begin? Will it pay out if they move into a retirement community, or do they have to remain in their home? How much, per day, does it cover, and is there a limit?

If there are concerns about paying for long-term care, either at home or in another setting, check into publicly funded programs. For Veterans, the V.A. may be able to help with their "Aid and Assistance Program." Call or e-mail any of the resources listed in the "Additional Resources" section in the back of this book. These organizations may be able to direct you to an appropriate source.

Placing someone in a facility can be a challenging decision for anyone to make. It's important to remind yourself that you are doing the best that you can, although, at times, it may never seem like enough. Communicate openly and honestly with your loved ones and have a good support system with family, friends, and clergy. Focus on any positive aspects and continuously make your aging loved ones feel part of the decision-making process. Take them along, if possible, when looking at different options in living arrangements. Make them feel like they are part of the process. Change is difficult, and this is not an easy time for anyone involved. Listen to what your loved ones have to say and remind them that if, after a period of time, they are unhappy somewhere, there are many other choices to explore together.

Adult Living Facilities Evaluation Form

The following is a suggested guide for you to make copies of and take with you while visiting and evaluating facilities with your loved ones.

Name of Facility: _____

Address: _____

Phone: _____ **Fax:** _____ **E-mail:** _____
Website: _____
Contact Person/Title: _____

Type of Facility: (Check Box)
Adult Day Care___   Hospice___
Acute Rehab___   Nursing Home___
Alzheimer's and Dementia___   Retirement and Independent___
Assisted Living___   Respite___
Continuing Care Retirement Community___

Size of Facility: (Number of apartments, rooms, etc.) _____

Appearance and Cleanliness of Facility: _____

Appearance and Demeanor of Staff: _____

Appearance, Demeanor and Cleanliness of Residents: _____

How often are the residents bathed? _____

How often are incontinence briefs or diapers changed? _____

Does the facility offer dietary restricted meals? _____

What are the guidelines for residents who need additional care? _____

What is the protocol when residents are near death? _____

Staff to Resident Ratio: Daytime _____ **Evening** _____

Amenities Offered: _____

Description of Costs: (Check Box)
Rental___ Purchase___
Equity___ Endowment___
Price: _____

Additional/Supplemental Costs: _____

Deposits: _____

Waiting List _____

Refund Policy _____

Payment Type: (Check Box)
Medicare   ____   Medicaid   ____
Private Pay ____   Private Insurance ____

Available Services: (Check Box)
Meals   ____   Transportation   ____   Housekeeping____
Laundry   ____   Maintenance   ____   Security   ____
Personal Care   ____   Social Activities   ____
Wellness Programs ____   Medication Management ____
Religious Activities ____   Medical Staff Therapy   ____
Other: _____
_____

Safety Features: _____
Emergency Provisions: _____
_____

Owner/Management Company: _____

Additional Comments/Information: _____
_____
_____

CHAPTER 2

WHEN YOUR LOVED ONE IS RESISTANT TO CHANGE

We all want the people we love and care about to be happy and safe. However, as our loved ones age, their safety and well being becomes more of an issue. They are fearful of losing their independence, and any assistance is viewed, through their eyes, as the beginning of the end. Withholding information about health issues, even to a medical professional, can be a common occurrence.

Sally's mother Edna had an appointment with her cardiologist. Although Sally usually takes time off from work to drive her mother to medical appointments, Edna refused her daughter's offer to drive her there. Edna didn't want her taking off from work again. Sally didn't want her mother to know that her productivity had been decreasing at work due to many daily phone calls from her mother. When Sally spoke to her mother later in the day, Edna was exhausted from waiting for the bus to take her and pick her up and from waiting at the doctor's office. Sally was frustrated and angry, and she felt like she had failed her mother. At the same time, she was torn because of her work obligations.

We like to think that our relationships with our aging loved ones will become better with time, but, more often than not, that is not the case. Finding ways to appreciate those relationships will help to break the cycle of strained relationships. Try engaging in activities that are pleasant or entertaining for both of you. This will help focus attention in the present as well as give everyone new memories to reminisce about later.

There is a delicate balance between helping those we love who are in need of assistance and trying to take care of other obligations, including our careers, other family members, and our own health. Many employers have resources to assist their employees with various family issues. Inquire through Human Resources or Employee Assistance Programs about possible solutions.

Be aware that, as situations develop and you address concerns, if you are not already hearing the following comments, you probably will. Here are some examples:

"I don't need anyone's help. I'm completely capable of doing things *on my own!*"

"I don't need to go to the doctor. There's *nothing wrong* with me."

"My driving is fine! You *are not* going to take my car keys from me."

What do you do? Here are a few tips:

- Try to understand that your loved ones are fearful of losing their independence. They want to do whatever they can to keep whatever remains. Reassure them. Don't resist them. When safety has become a main concern, enlist the help of a professional. A physician, clergy member, or close friend can help convince them to accept assistance. To a certain degree, be flexible when resistance is occurring. Here are some examples of things you might say:

"Mom, if we have someone help out with errands, prepare meals, and do some housekeeping, you and I can spend more quality time together. *Let's just try it* a few times and see how it goes. Do this for me, okay?"
This approach eases your loved one into having help.

"Dad, living in (a retirement community, assisted living …) you have *the option of participating* in social activities only if you want to." In this scenario, show your loved ones there are options to engaging in activities. Chances are, over time, if they see all the socialization taking place, they will begin to engage in activities and enjoy themselves as well.

- How you phrase your comments and concerns is important. You will have better success when you state your needs instead of stressing their needs and what they should or should not do. Here's an example:

"It will make us feel better if we know someone is here in the morning while you take a shower—someone to remind you to take all your medications. Then you can have the rest of the day *to do as you please*. It's only for a few hours." In this example, the emphasis is on your needs versus their needs. Starting with a few hours each day, or several days a week, eases them into the situation.

• It is not your job to control your loved ones' lives. Your top priority should be their health, safety, and well-being. Could they possibly be endangering their lives or someone else's? Continue to reinforce any independence that may remain. An example follows with suggestions for how to approach the situation in conversation.

Much to David's dismay, his father, Jack, 82, is still driving. When David went to pick his father up the other day to have dinner, he noticed a significant dent in the back fender of his father's new car. Previous conversations about Jack's driving have gotten nowhere. David knows it is now time to take further action before something happens and someone gets hurt. Here's what he told his father:

"Dad, I've made an appointment to take you for a driving test. We all know that other people drive very defensively. We want to make sure your reflexes are all right, so you can be safe. There might be some things we can learn to do so you can continue to drive."

Another approach can be to get a third party involved. Sometimes they can be more sensitive to the elderly person's desire to maintain independence. Continuously let them know you want to work with them, not against them. You can even try keeping the conversation light by saying: "Mom, with this traffic and the way people drive, personally, I would *love* someone to drive me around."

You may need to limit their driving in the beginning. Make sure someone can be in the car with them, if at all possible. Only allow them to drive during the daytime and for short distances. If someone else has earned their trust and is gradually allowed to drive them places, they should become accustomed to the situation.

A senior's independence is directly correlated with being able to drive. As we all age, we have a decrease in cognitive capacity. Elderly persons can drift into other lanes, have a decrease in response time, or have more difficulty seeing at night. A brain-to-muscle breakdown occurs and causes slowing movements and stiffness.

Upon completing tests, physicians can notify the Department of Motor Vehicles if it is not safe for someone to drive.

AAA has many resources for senior drivers to assist them with their driving skills. The goal is safety and being proactive, not to restrict driving. AAA has developed an interactive DVD that evaluates physical, mental, and visual driving skills. It identifies potential weaknesses through eight functional areas and helps to possibly strengthen those weaknesses. Contact www.AAA.com or call their customer service department at 1-800-891-4222. Other resources include www.seniordrivers.org or www.aarp.org.

If you haven't raised certain issues with them, ask yourself why not? What's stopping you? Is it a fear within yourself? Are you afraid they will get angry and start an argument?

If that happens to be the case, get someone involved who has the respect of your loved one whether it's a friend, a clergy member, or a medical professional. This may take the pressure off of you and relieve any hesitancy you may have.

Have you made a conscious decision to leave an issue alone because it is in your parents' best interests? Or because you prefer to avoid discussing it?

Weigh the cost of raising concerns against not bringing them up. Getting advice from someone who has lived through this can help lessen the guilt and frustration that everyone involved is experiencing.

Remember, most people wait until they are in a crisis mode before doing anything. That may not be the best time for making decisions!

- Discuss the risks and benefits of what may be happening. If your loved ones have difficulty walking up or down a flight of stairs, can arrangements be made for living rooms/bedrooms/bathrooms to be on the main floor, or can a chair lift be installed? If loved ones can no longer cook for themselves, can meals be delivered? Meals-On-Wheels, non-profit organizations, and religious groups are a great resource for this service. Many schools require teens to participate in community service activities.

- If you don't live close by, can someone from church, a student, or retired neighbor volunteer to drive your loved ones to the store, hair salon, bank, or wherever they need to go? Make your parents an active part of the solution. Include them in as many decisions as possible. If they cannot balance their checkbooks, or if they forget to pay bills, will they grant power of attorney, for financial matters, to a relative, an accountant, or a lawyer?

- Ask your parents, depending on the issue, to try something a few times. They will generally become accustomed to being around people in adult day care, having the right caregiver in their home, or living in a senior community.

- By visiting several facilities with them, you can show your parents how the residents interact and have fun. Try to schedule visits when there are activities such as bingo, arts and crafts, or sing-alongs occurring. If you see something on the activities schedule that you know your parents enjoy, make sure your visit is during that time.

Go slow. Ease your loved ones into the change. Go together on several visits to different facilities. Ask them what their opinion is so they feel part of the decision-making process. Adult caregivers of the aging often think they know what has to be done and what needs to happen quickly. If you haven't waited until the situation is out of hand, be patient and tolerant of their opinion. Give your parents several choices. Direct the conversation to options, not "yes" or "no" answers.

- If you are facing a very difficult situation and still don't know where to turn, involve someone who has the respect of the senior. Get help from a physician, a clergy member, a close friend, or a geriatric care consultant. Explore the options available within your company through Employee Assistance Programs and Human Resource Programs.

Remember, it's not about reducing your loved ones' quality of life, it's about increasing it!

CHAPTER 3

OPTIONS IN CARE AND LIVING ARRANGEMENTS

As they age, most individuals wish to remain in their own homes. For many, it can decrease the worry and expense of moving into a senior care facility. However, remaining at home can cause serious issues if health challenges are not managed or monitored. This chapter outlines the pros and cons of various options in living arrangements.

> **Before finalizing any living arrangements, check with a legal advisor and/or tax advisor when any contracts or legal documents require a signature or a deposit.**

I cannot overemphasize the importance of the information in the textbox. You should never sign legal documents or pay deposits without consulting with a legal advisor or tax advisor. This is simply for your own protection.

Should Your Aging Parent Move In With You?

Since Alice and Jim have lived in their home for almost 60 years, it's understandable that they want to stay there for as long as possible. After consulting with their physician and accountant, Alice and Jim have agreed to hire a caregiver to come help and them seven days a week for 6 hours a day to start. Alice will continue to drive, but only on a limited basis. She has agreed that when she's not feeling up to it, she will allow the caregiver to drive for her. Jim's long-term care policy will reimburse them when the caregiver begins services. As Jim's Alzheimer's disease progresses, the family will explore facilities for both of their parents. Alice and Jim don't want to be separated. Although

their financial resources seem significant, careful consideration needs to be given to sell-
ing their assets, including their house, car, stocks and bonds, over time.

Older people want to live their lives to the fullest as long as they are able. They don't want anyone to assume their judgment is impaired just because their mobility is declining. Older adults are usually willing to make life easier on others, but not at the cost of their independence.

If you make the decision to become a caregiver to an elderly person and have them move into your home, a new dynamic occurs. You are now in charge of that person. He or she is not in charge of you, as it might have been when you were a child. The adjustment is severe, especially for the caregiver if he or she also cares for children.

This can be a time when extreme tension is experienced by everyone involved. A sense of balance can be restored to the relationship when you openly talk to one another about issues such as needs, expectations, and setting boundaries.

When considering whether it makes sense to have aging parents live with adult children, take into account the following:

- First clarify your expectations and your parents' expectations in a discussion with them.

    Do your parents want to live with one of their children, alone, or in a retirement community?

    Do you have sufficient financial resources to receive your parents?

    Is your house designed and equipped for them to live with you?

    Will they have to climb stairs?

    Can safety features be installed in their bathroom?

    Is there a separate living area for them to allow for privacy?

    How does the rest of the family feel about having your parents move in?

    How much time can be devoted to the caregiving role?

- To help share the responsibility and to decrease stress levels, other people such as a spouse, children, brothers, sisters, other relatives, and friends should be involved. Ask for assistance and set up a schedule of who is available on what days and evenings to help out. Get others to commit to helping with certain activities. This gives the primary caregiver time for personal activities and other commitments.

- If everyone is working full-time and has other responsibilities, inquire within your company to find out if it is feasible for you to cut back on work hours, change to job sharing, use flex-time, telecommute or try other alternatives in order to accommodate this new arrangement.

- Make a list of expenses and determine how much the parent, caregiver, and other family members will contribute. Sometimes, elder parents will have resources, for example, from the sale of their house, car, stocks and bonds, pensions, money market accounts, or other assets which will help to pay the full cost of their care.

- Find out about the tax breaks available to caregivers. You may be able to claim the parent as a dependent. Check with a financial advisor for details. The savings can be significant. In situations where several siblings provide support to an aging parent, but none provides more than half, usually only one can claim an exemption.

Should everyone agree to this living arrangement, remember to have patience, allow everyone time to adjust to the new situation, and choose your battles.

If after giving this a considerable amount of time to work, and it's causing a strain on your marriage or your career or causing you health problems, seek counseling, if necessary. Take action before the situation gets out of control. Plan and coordinate in advance. This way, many issues can be resolved quickly.

And, remember, flexibility and teamwork is key for all involved. If, after a trial basis, the arrangement doesn't work, there are many other options to consider.

Respite Care

As caregivers, family members often need a break from care giving. At times, we need reminders to take breaks for ourselves. Taking breaks benefits those we take care of. Set aside time on a regular basis for yourself. This is healthy and necessary. Respite care is provided in or out of the home. Personal in-home care services are available for to relieve caregivers. Adult day care centers offer daytime hours of care, activities, and limited medical needs. For care over longer periods of time, many assisted living facilities offer respite care for several days or weeks at a time.

With costs for a monthly stay at major assisted living facilities ranging from approximately $2,500 to $6,000 a month, it's important to check the facts to determine your needs and the needs of your loved one.

Mike's dad, Ed, is 83 and lives with his son. Ed is in early stages of Alzheimer's disease. Friends from their church check in on Ed during the day and often bring him lunch. There are occasions when Mike has to travel for work and is gone overnight, sometimes several days at a time. He's concerned about leaving his father alone now that Ed is waking up in the middle of the night and wandering around the house, a symptom of Alzheimer's. Mike is considering hiring a caregiver agency on an "as needed" basis when he travels. He is also planning to take a much-needed vacation in a few months. One of the options he and his father are discussing together is to try a brief stay in an assisted living facility while Mike is away. They're looking at several places that also have Alzheimer's care so that when the time comes, they will have a place for Ed to eventually live. By handling things this way, it eases both of them into changes that will need to be made, and Ed gets a chance to become accustomed to a particular place, its residents and staff.

You Should Consider Respite Care When:

- Adult children need to travel for business or take a much-needed break from caregiving.

- Your elderly parent needs to transfer from one location to another or is visiting for an extended length of time.

- Help is needed with daily activities of living following a hospitalization, injury, or illness.

- Your parent wants to be in at home while undergoing intense medical treatment, such as chemotherapy, and daily obligations are overwhelming.

Questions to Ask and What to Look for
When Considering Respite Care:

1. Look for a facility that best suits your parents' needs in terms of healthcare, socialization, and the comforts of home.

2. Ask if there is a minimum stay and about health requirements and all fees including add-on costs.

3. Financially determine the costs of staying at the facility versus having your loved one live with you or having an agency/caregiver come to them during this time.

4. Speak with a financial advisor about any tax deductions associated with any of these expenses. The best source is an accountant or tax expert.

5. Should you and your parents decide on respite care in an assisted living facility, make sure to take a few personal possessions such as pictures, plants, and blankets/comforters to make their surroundings feel like home.

Where to Find a Respite Care Facility:

- Ask a hospital discharge planner, social worker, or case manager.

- Refer to the previous sections on In-Home Care and Assisted Living.

- Search the Internet using the following keywords: respite care facilities, assisted living facilities, short-term care, in-home personal care.

Home Care Agencies & Private Hire Caregivers

Today, there are many personal home care services that are available to seniors. They help provide for their comfort and independence, while insuring their medical well-being and security.

This type of care may include either state-licensed agencies or private individuals who provide services in the home such as assistance with tasks like bathing, dressing, giving medication reminders, taking vital signs, changing bandages, preparing meals, and providing light housekeeping and transportation.

In-home caregivers allow the seniors to remain in their own home with flexible care options. If you decide to hire a home care agency or private duty caregiver, careful attention should be given to the hiring process.

There are distinct advantages to hiring a caregiver through a home care agency. Most agencies carry liability insurance, perform all reference and background checks on workers, handle payment to caregivers, and guarantee backup care. You should be aware, however, that agencies may require you to use a minimum number of hours. The standard is usually a minimum of 3–4 hours per day.

If you hire a caregiver privately, the burden of finding, interviewing, and background-checking caregivers is your responsibility. So is payment (which may involve calculating taxes and social security) and locating backup care. On the plus side, performing interviews yourself can be a good way to find the right person.

Consider a Home Care Agency or Private Hire When:

- The senior needs assistance with his daily activities such as showering, dressing, or remembering to take medications.

- When elderly persons can no longer drive, we should be alert to the possibility of a need for change. This is especially true if they are unstable on their feet, have difficulty rising from a bed or chair, or have fallen.

- Memory issues are further signs. If people become disoriented or lost while walking or driving, or just around the house, they need care.

- When seniors cannot function independently and should not be left alone.

Questions to Ask When Considering Home Care:

1. Is the agency or individual licensed, bonded, or insured?

2. What services do they provide? Personal care? Housekeeping? Meal preparation? Transportation?

3. Do they offer in-home assessments? If so, is there a fee? How much?

4. Explain your loved ones' situation and ask for an opinion. What do they recommend? This is also the time to get opinions from trained healthcare professionals—social workers, geriatric care managers, and physicians.

5. What is the staff's medical training and background?

6. Does a client always get the same caregiver? It is preferable to have continuity and develop a relationship with the caregiver. Alzheimer's and dementia patients, in particular, need consistency to avoid additional confusion.

7. What are the costs? Is there a minimum number of hours? Are there discounts for longer hours?

8. What types of insurance do they accept?

Ask for references from the agency or individual. In the case of a private duty caregiver, be extremely thorough. Ask for the names, addresses, phone numbers, and dates of employment for previous employers. Be sure to contact them. Check with your local State Department of Human Resources for any complaints/incidents/reports that may have been registered against the agency or individual.

Where to Find a Home Care Agency:

Contact a Geriatric Case Manager, www.caremanager.org will direct you to a list in your area.

Hospitals may offer lists of discharge planners or social workers.

National Association of Area Agency on Aging, 1-202-872-0888. www.n4a.org.

Eldercare Locator, 1-800-677-1116, ww.eldercare.gov.

Retirement Communities—Ask the marketing director, director of nursing, or executive director.

Some churches or synagogues provide lists of agencies or private duty caregivers.

Word of mouth—Ask people who may have used a home care agency in the past or know someone who has or is currently using one.

Search the Internet—Try these key words: caregiver agencies, eldercare, adult home care, senior home caregivers.

Home Healthcare Companies

Home Health Care Companies are different from Home Care Agencies. Home Health Companies are Medicare-certified to provide skilled nursing services which include physical therapy and speech therapy in the home for treatment of an illness or an injury. A physician must provide direction in the type of care required. This may include nursing care, therapy, or skilled nursing care. Usually, this is done after hospitalization or surgery, injury, or illness.

To qualify for Medicare Home Health Coverage, you must meet all of the following requirements:

1. A physician determines that the patient needs in-home care.

2. The care includes periodic (not full-time) skilled care, physical therapy, or speech therapy and has a limited number of visits. Each visit generally lasts 30–60 minutes.

3. The patient must be homebound, unable to leave home without considerable effort and leaving home only to attend doctor's appointments, hair appointments, or for short rides in the car or short walks.

4. The Home Health Company must be Medicare-approved.

Security and Medical Alert Devices

During those times when your elderly parents are home alone, it is important for everyone's peace of mind and your parents' safety to consider having medical alerts and security devices. They allow for assistance in the event of falls, illness, a home invasion, or any emergency.

Pam works full time. Her mother, Carol, lives with her and has diabetes, chronic obstructive pulmonary disease (COPD), and severe rheumatoid arthritis. She uses oxygen equipment at all times. There have been occasions, while Pam was at work, when her mother has fallen and been unable to get up. Carol had difficulty getting to the phone to call someone to help her. Their financial resources are limited; however, Pam and her mother are exploring options to get additional help. In the meantime, Pam has bought her mother a security necklace to wear in case of an emergency.

These items can be purchased through medical equipment supply stores or companies and many retail pharmacies. Often, these stores are located in or around a hospital. You can also purchase or order walkers, scooters, wheelchairs, gait belts, hoyer lifts, raised toilet seats, shower chairs, grab bars, and much more.

Payment is generally private pay, but in some circumstances, with a written prescription from a physician, Medicare Part B may help cover these supplies.

Medical Equipment for Mobility

There are many choices to consider regarding mobility within and outside the home. An assessment of needs should be made by a professional, such as a case manager or social worker. Items to consider are:

- Wheelchairs

- Power wheelchairs

- Scooters

- Ramps

- Vans

- Equipment for transportation

- Transfer equipment

- Patient lifts

- Stair chair lifts

Medicare Part B may cover part expenses if the patient meets the criteria. Otherwise, payment is private pay.

Adult Day Care

Adult day care offers seniors a safe, structured environment during daytime hours where they participate in a variety of programs and social activities such as games, outings, and arts and crafts. In many cases, meals and snacks are served throughout the day.

Now that Alice and Jim will have a caregiver coming into their home, Alice will have some time to go to the local senior center. Their neighbors participate in activities at the center, and Alice has been wanting to take a computer class there. This will allow Alice to take a much-needed break from taking care of her husband, and she will be able to socialize with others. She can leave the house knowing that Jim is being attended to.

Some adult day care centers offer nursing, nutritional, and rehabilitation services on the premises, or can refer you to professionals in the community. Many adult day services can help people with disabilities live at home and postpone or avoid nursing home or assisted living care. The centers provide respite to caregivers and family members who juggle work and family with caregiver responsibilities during working hours.

Most adult day services are a private-pay option. However, if a center offers a particular service that meets Medicare requirements, such as physical or speech therapy, the program may reimburse for that particular service. Here are some definitions to help you explain the differences in **Medicare** and **Medicaid**:

- Medicare—a federal health insurance program for people age 65 and older, certain people under 65 with disabilities, and certain people with kidney disease. Eligibility depends on age or disability only.

- Medicaid—a program of health coverage administered by the states, for certain people with low incomes or very high medical bills. Eligibility depends on age, disability, or family status *and* on an individual's (or family's) income and resources.

Adult day care centers are usually privately-owned, operated by the county government, or by a religious organization. The charges are hourly, weekly or monthly. There are several types of adult day care centers:

- The Social Model—for the active, independent senior. These individuals are able to function physically and emotionally on their own. Social models provide food, activities, and supervision of seniors during daytime hours. Transportation may or may not be provided.

- The Medical Model—for those individuals who are impaired physically and/or cognitively, need assistance with personal care and medications, or who do not need 24-hour supervision, but cannot function independently during the day. This model, if approved under a community care program, may have services reimbursed by Medicaid. Alzheimer's programs are included in the medical model. They are generally funded by the state through the Area Agency on Aging (AAA) or through charitable donations of religious organizations.

You Should Consider Adult Day Care if a Senior:

- Is unable to structure his activities or schedule daily events.

- Desires or needs the companionship of others, as well as mental stimulation.

- Cannot fully function independently and should not be left alone.

Questions to Consider

There are many questions you should ask before placing your loved one in adult day care. Finding answers to the questions below will help you assess the quality of a day care facility.

1. Who owns, operates, and sponsors the facility?

    In some states, adult day care facilities are not regulated by the state or subject to audits. Contact your state's Department of Human Services or State Ombudsman's Office regarding questions you have or to find out about any reports of abusive treatment.

2. Is the center state-licensed?

    Some states do not require Adult Day Care facilities to have a state license. If that is the case, do your homework! Check references, call the Better Business Bureau, and make several unexpected visits to observe the staff and to see the patients' behavior.

3. How long have they been in business?

    This establishes credibility and will assist you in checking references and reports from state organizations.

4. Check with the Health Department for any complaints against the center.

5. What are the days and hours of operation?

6. Is there transportation provided to and from the home? Is there a charge for this? If so, how much?

7. What is the cost? Hourly rates? Weekly? Monthly?

8. Are there extra costs such as healthcare or meals? Do they provide dietary restricted meals such as low sodium or diabetic food?

9. Do they accept Medicare, Medicaid, or private insurance? If so, what is the procedure for filing claims for reimbursements?

10. What are the health conditions of patients that they will and will not accept? Do they accept incontinent patients, Alzheimer's patients, and/or wheelchair patients?

11. Are there any restrictions on the patients they have?

12. Is there a waiting list?

13. What services are provided for those with Alzheimer's or related dementias?

14. Ask for a copy of their meal plan and activity schedule. See if your loved one and you can eat a meal there before you decide to sign up for the center.

15. Is the facility clean and odorless?

16. Is the furniture comfortable and pleasant to use for an entire day? Are there loungers and reclining chairs for relaxation?

17. What is the staff to patient ratio? This provides you with an idea of the amount of attention patients will receive.

18. Is there a separate area for someone who gets ill while at the center? What do they do when someone gets sick? Is there a registered nurse on staff? Will the nurse give injections of medications and pills throughout the day? Find out what they will and will not do in terms of medical service.

Where to Find Adult Daycare Centers:

National Adult Day Services, 1-800-558-5301, www.nadsa.org.

Eldercare Locator, 1-800-677-1116, www.eldercare.gov.

Administration on Aging, (202) 619-0724, www.aoa.gov.

AARP, 1-888-687-2277, www.aarp.org.

Alzheimer's Association, 1-800-272-3900, www.alz.org.

Geriatric Case Managers, www.caremanagers.org.

Check with local churches or synagogues.

Check the Internet or Yellow Pages for these keywords: adult daycare centers, aging services, senior citizen services.

Acute Rehabilitation

Acute rehabilitation takes place as a direct result of a stay in the hospital. The hospital stay can be due to anything from broken bones, surgery, or strokes. Facilities focus on personalizing the patient's ability to regain functionality. There are teams of specialists including physicians, nurses, and speech, occupational, and physical therapists for various areas of convalescence. Social workers, dieticians, recreational therapists, chaplains, and psychologists are also readily available.

Each facility has criteria that must be met before a patient is admitted. This is evaluated and determined by a physician, discharge planner, attending nurse, or other healthcare professional at the hospital. The expectation is for improvement so that the patients can resume function after they leave. The patients must be willing to participate in as much as 3–5 hours of therapy per day.

If a patient is not a candidate for acute rehab, the family/caregiver may qualify for a two-week family teaching stay. This is strictly for the purposes of educating the caregiver in how to properly take care of their loved one once the patient goes home. Arrangements are made for any services, including home health care visits or delivery of medical supplies and equipment.

Questions to Ask and Considerations for Acute Rehab:

1. Generally, Medicare pays for all or most of the stay. Find out from the physician and the facility what is covered. Supplemental insurance will generally pay for the remaining amount. Check with them as well. Otherwise, the remainder is private pay.

2. Check out several facilities and ask to take a tour. Bed availability may limit any choices.

3. Look for patients who are clean and attended to.

4. Is the facility odorless and clean?

5. Do they have activities scheduled each day for the patients? Ask to see a calendar of events.

6. Determine through meeting with specialists whether any educational information or classes are given for the family.

7. Is there group or one-on-one therapy? Are you able to observe anyone receiving physical therapy, for example, while you are there?

8. Ask to see the schedule of events and a meal at the facility. Do they offer dietary restricted meals?

Where to Find an Acute Rehab Facility

Get recommendations from the hospital physician, attending nurse, discharge planner, social worker, or case manager.

Ask a church or synagogue for several references.

If you know of someone who has gone through this with a loved one, a personal referral is a good choice.

Search online under the following keywords: acute rehabilitation facilities, skilled nursing home, respite care.

Retirement/Independent Living

Living in an independent/retirement living environment is for persons who no longer want the responsibility of maintaining a home but are fully capable of living an independent lifestyle. A social atmosphere is created for people in the same age range who come together for similar interests. Residents have freedom and privacy within a convenient, comfortable atmosphere in addition to increased security with relief from household obligations.

Some independent living facilities offer many activities including swimming pools/spas, exercise facilities, libraries, restaurants, and hair salons. Laundry/linen services and local transportation may also be available.

This level of residence is private pay only.

Consider a Retirement Community When:

- Your loved one wants freedom, increased security, privacy, and a social environment. Standard safety features are available. No medical staff is in on-site; however, wellness programs may be offered.

- Your parents prefer to live around people within their age ranges and want to remain active with social and recreational activities (usually starting at 55 years of age and older).

- Your loved ones want to have the option of eating in their residence or in a restaurant located within the facility and when housekeeping assistance is helpful.

- Your loved ones may still drive, but would like to have transportation available for shopping, outside entertainment, and activities.

Questions to Ask When Considering Independent Living Communities:

1. What restrictions do they have in relation to age, medical status, and physical function?

2. What safety features are available in each apartment?

3. What are the costs, including deposits, amenities, and any miscellaneous fees?

4. Is there any type of medical facility on the property? Is there nurse available to check vital signs and monitor medications?

5. What are the activities planned? Ask to see a monthly calendar of events.

6. Ask to see menus from the restaurant and have a meal there with your parent.

7. Ask to take a tour of the property. Assess the residents. Are they active, and do they appear to be in good health?

8. If a resident moves out, what portion, if any, of the deposit is refunded? And to whom?

Where to Find Independent Retirement Communities:

Check local magazines and periodicals. Often, independent communities advertise in these types of media.

Check with a church or synagogue for a list of places in the area where your parent wants to live.

AARP, 1-888-687-2277, www.aarp.org.

Enlist the help of a geriatric case manager in the particular area of interest, www.casemanager.org.

Contact the National Association of Area Agency on Aging, 202-872-0888, www.n4a.org.

Assisted Living and Personal Care Homes

Assisted Living and Personal Care facilities serve residents who are becoming decreasingly capable of independence. They offer various levels of supervision and assistance. Staffs generally include medically trained personnel. The facilities are meant to fill the gap between independent living and a nursing home. The government does not regulate these facilities. However, various licensing categories are used for them.

Within the next few months, Mary is planning on taking Alice and Jim to visit several assisted living properties that include Alzheimer's areas. In this type of setting, Alice can still visit her husband and have meals with him in the Alzheimer's dining room. Alice's needs will be attended to as well.

Many seniors living in active retirement communities, or in their own homes, have developed a close circle of friends and neighbors. When health issues arise, they rely on one another to help out. Although the intention is always good, not everyone is fully capable or in the position to be of assistance. When this becomes a problem, seniors should take note and begin discussing other options such as assisted living facilities.

The facilities have trained staff members available to help residents with daily routines such as showering, dressing, and medication reminders. Housekeeping and laundry services are also available. An activities director arranges on- and off-site events involving entertainment and shopping.

Medicare and Medicaid do not pay for these facilities. Some long-term care insurance policies offer reimbursement for this service. This is discussed later in the book.

You Should Consider Assisted Living/PCHs when:

- Your elderly parents need help in an emergency.

- Stand-by assistance may be needed, such as reminders to take medications, bathing assistance, incontinence assistance, meal preparation, housekeeping, and laundry services.

- Encouragement is needed to participate in activities.

- Your elderly parents have mild or moderate memory impairment, are confused, or disoriented.

- The family has some concerns, and something needs to be done quickly.

Questions to Ask when Considering an Assisted Living Facility/Personal Care Home:

1. Are there any restrictions on the types of patients they admit?

2. What services are provided for the basic rate and each level of service needed? What does each service cost?

3. Do the residents look clean, and are they dressed in clean clothes?

4. Are there skilled nurses on staff who are trained and licensed to administer medications and injections? Is there a medical director? Are physical therapy and other therapies offered?

5. Are religious services available?

6. Is there adequate staff? What is the ratio of staff to residents? What is the ratio at night?

7. Ask to eat a meal there with your parent. Ask to see a weekly menu. Do they allow for dietary restrictions such as low sodium, diabetic, and kosher meals? Do they serve snacks? Are the residents assisted with eating when required?

8. Is there an activity program and a director? Ask to see a sample of their monthly calendar of events. Are there activities for residents who are visually impaired or confined to their apartments/rooms?

9. Are there a lot of people sitting around with nothing to do? Is there a main television area with good reception?

10. Do they provide transportation?

11. Will they provide references from current residents and their family members?

Where to Find Assisted Living/PCH Properties:

- Call your local hospital and ask the patient care coordinator department, case managers, or discharge planners for resources available in the area desired.

- Geriatric Case Managers, www.casemanager.org.

- Eldercare Locator, 1-800-677-1116, www.eldercare.gov.

- AARP, 1-888-687-2277, www.aarp.org.

- Check with local churches or synagogues.

- Search the Internet under keywords—assisted living facilities, residential care personal care, or adult congregate

Alzheimer's/Dementia Care

Many assisted living communities and nursing homes offer care for those with Alzheimer's disease and other related memory disorders. However, there are facilities now specializing in these types of patients. Reality-oriented programs are designed by a specially trained staff to the diminish confusion and agitation of the residents.

Buildings are designed to address problems associated with the disease with color-coded hallways. An array of visual cues is present in order to lessen complexities. Areas are secured to prevent residents from wandering off. Residents may wear a bracelet that sets off an alarm if they try to leave a particular area. Alarm systems are in place throughout the facility, should the resident try to open a door they should not open. Gates and fences should surround the property. Windows in rooms are be secured. The staff needs to observe residents' use of forks, knives, or other sharp objects.

Each stage of illness requires different levels of care and support. More advanced stages usually require 24-hour care including IV medications, physical therapy, speech therapy, wound care, and tube feedings.

Assistance by trained staff is available to help with grooming, dressing, personal hygiene, medication administration, and other daily activities. Meals, laundry services, and housekeeping are provided.

Most of these facilities are private pay only; however, veterans' insurance and long term care insurance may pay a portion of these costs. Medicare and Medicaid do not pay for this specialized care. However, they do pay for other skilled nursing care to be reviewed in the next section.

Questions to Ask When Considering an Alzheimer's/Dementia Facility:

1. Consult with the patient's physician, geriatric care manager, or trained healthcare professional to ask when an Alzheimer's facility is appropriate or necessary. Tests will determine what stage of the illness the patient is in and whether there are any other concerns that need to be addressed.

2. Ask for a copy of their fee schedule with a description of costs, including a breakdown of costs for each level of care as the illness progresses.

3. Ask about the availability of beds and living arrangements.

4. Make an appointment for a tour and visit at least 3–4 facilities. Schedule tours during "activities" and/or meal time.

5. Ask what rating the facility received by the state in its most recent review, as well as for several years back.

6. Ask for a copy of their "Residents Bill of Rights"

7. Check to make sure residents are safe, clean, and in a secure environment.

8. What provisions are in place for safety to prevent wandering off? Do residents have easy access to all areas? They should not!

9. Ask for an activity schedule and meal schedule

10. Are there various activities depending on each level of care?

11. Check with the Health Department for any complaints registered against the facility.

12. Ask to check references or speak directly with other families who have relatives living there. Schedule a private meeting to ask about any issues that may have caused problems.

13. Look for the attitude of management and staff. Does the staff and administration demonstrate compassion, affection and kindness toward residents?

14. Inquire about staff training and the ratio of staff to residents both during the day and evening shifts.

15. Are there educational classes to help families cope with illness? Are there support groups?

Where to Find Alzheimer's/Dementia Facilities:

• The Alzheimer's Association, www.alzfdn.org, 1-800-272-3900.

• A local hospital discharge planner, case manager, social worker, or a family physician.

• Eldercare Locator, 1-800-677-1116, www.eldercarelocator.gov.

• Contact a geriatric care manager, www.caremanager.org.

• Check churches or synagogues for local resources

• Check online or in the yellow pages under the following key words: Alzheimer's living facilities, assisted living, memory care facilities.

Nursing Homes/Skilled Nursing Facilities

Nursing homes are designed for those individuals who require 24-hour nursing care. They employ R.N.s (registered nurses), L.P.N.s (licensed practical nurses) and C.N.A.s (certified nursing assistants) to care for the chronically ill who are no longer able to stay at home, in assisted living, or in independent retirement communities.

Skilled nursing homes provide many of the same amenities as other facilities including room, personal care/hygiene, medication administration, meals, laundry, and cleaning services.

Medical services include rehabilitation, tube feedings, and IV medication. Speech, respiratory, and physical therapists are on staff. All activities are encouraged within the individual patient's health status.

Nursing homes are state-licensed and are regulated and reviewed by state departments of public health. Each facility is certified by the state for Medicare and Medicaid. A basic daily or monthly fee is charged. Inquire about financial responsibility. You can sometimes arrange for financial assistance when planning ahead. Consult with the director of the nursing home, who can be a great resource to guide you through the proper channels for any help you may need.

Long term care insurance, Medicare, Medicaid, private insurance, and private funds pay for this level of care. The nursing home will ask for financial information in order to determine the appropriate payment source.

Many nursing homes also offer acute rehabilitative services. These patients are housed in a separate area from the long-term residents.

When to Consider a Skilled Nursing Home:

- When your loved one can no longer function at home, in assisted living or in independent living and must have 24-hour medical supervision.

- When the individual's overall health, medical, and physical needs can no longer be met by those currently attending to them.

Questions to Ask When Considering Skilled Nursing:

1. Ask for a copy of their reviews from the Division of Licensing and Regulation and the Office of the Inspector General. Each year, when surveyed by the state, they should receive a superior rating.

2. Set up an appointment to visit at least 3–4 facilities. If possible, take the elderly person with you.

3. Are they certified for Medicare, Medicaid, or other types of insurance? What is their procedure for this?

4. Is the facility well-maintained? Odorless? Clean?

5. Are the residents attended to or left by themselves in the hallways? Are they clean?

6. What types of medical meal plans are offered?

7. What is the staff to patient ratio during both the day and evening shifts?

8. What is the general attitude of the staff? Do they appear friendly, courteous, and considerate of patients?

9. What types of therapies are available to residents?

10. What activities do they have? Ask for a calendar of events.

11. Is clergy available? If so, when are they available?

12. What restrictions, if any, are there for staying in and being admitted to the home?

13. Are emergency call buttons located next to the beds and in the bathrooms?

Where to Find Skilled Nursing Facilities:

- Your hospital discharge planner, social worker, case manager, attending nurse, or physician.

- Call a reputable home health care company for referrals.

- Check with a church or synagogue for referrals.

- Administration on Aging, 1-202-619-0724, www.aoa.gov.

- Eldercare Locator, 1-800-677-1666, www.eldercare.gov.

- A geriatric care manager in the geographic area of interest, www.caremanager.org.

- Talk with anyone you know who has dealt with skilled nursing facilities. Word of mouth is an excellent resource.

Continuing Care Retirement Communities

Continuing Care Retirement Communities (CCRCs) provide an entire spectrum of living choices, all on the same property. They provide a continuum of care from private homes and independent living apartments to assisted living, memory care, and skilled nursing suites. The benefit of CCRCs is that individuals can age in a place without having to relocate. Housing is provided, no matter what the medical needs may be. Inquire about any constraints should a resident require additional care and assistance. If a property does not have additional staffing included for one-on-one care, extra costs may be incurred by the resident.

In order to live in a CCRC, residents may or may not have to buy into the property. The fee may be refundable should the resident decide to move out or upon death. In some cases, the deposit can be put into an escrow account for future healthcare. Find out about refundable fees should the resident decide to move.

In CCRCs, a monthly payment covers rent, meals, services, amenities, and/ or medical care. Many times, the community will have requirements in order for residents to live there. These can be based on age, income, health status, and/or financial assets.

Discuss the geographic desirability and expenses of *any* type of retirement community. Is living too far away going to hinder visits? If the elderly person becomes ill, can extra help be afforded, or will this create a financial burden?

Alice, Jim, and their family are talking about eventually moving into a continuing care retirement community. There are several within an hour's drive from their daughter Mary's home. As Jim's Alzheimer's disease progresses, he can live in the memory support area of a community, and Alice can live in the assisted living area of the property. They can still be in the same building and be able to visit and eat meals together. Their other option is to live in an assisted living facility that also has an Alzheimer's unit in the building.

When to Consider a Continuing Care Retirement Community:

- When the elderly individual prefers to age in one place without having to relocate.

- When various types of housing are separated, yet on the same property, no matter what the residents' medical needs.

Questions to Ask When Considering CCRCs:

1. What are the costs? Do you buy-in to the property?

2. What restrictions do they have?

3. Is the fee refundable and, if so, at what point? If your parent chooses to move out or passes away, how much of the deposit will be refunded and to whom?

4. Ask for a tour of the facility. See what the resident's health condition is in each section (independent, assisted, memory care, skilled nursing)

5. Ask to eat a meal there with your parent. Is food available for dietary restrictions such as low-sodium and diabetic diets?

6. What social activities take place for each level of care? Do they have off-site activities?

7. Are the residents in memory care or skilled nursing being attended to? Are they kept clean?

8. What is the staff to resident ratio in the higher levels of care? What about at night?

9. What types of transportation are available? If someone has a doctor's appointment, how is transportation arranged?

10. Speak with some of the residents, if possible, or with their family members regarding the quality of care, level of service, and pros and cons of the community.

Where to Find CCRCs:

- Many religious affiliations have these communities. In most cases, you do not have to be a member of a particular denomination in order to live in the communities.

- Eldercare Locator, 1-800-677-1116, www.eldercare.gov.

- AARP, 1-888-687-2277, www.aarp.org.

- Geriatric Care Managers, www.caremanagers.org.

- Check local magazines for advertisements and in the Sunday newspaper in the area of choice. This will give you an idea of the overall aesthetics of the properties.

- Search online using the following keywords: continuing care retirement communities, independent and assisted living communities.

Hospice Care

Hospice Services can help lessen the physical, emotional, and spiritual discomforts of patients in the final phases of their lives. Families and friends may also benefit from the accompanying peace of mind hospice care brings. The focus shifts from a curative method to comfort and quality of life care. Pain management and comfort are the key factors of hospice or palliative care.

Hospice cares for patients in their homes, nursing homes, assisted living communities, or in-patient hospice facilities.

Teams of skilled professionals are available to the patient and family to provide services for end of life care. Supportive care is also offered to caregivers and families of the hospice patient. Through comfort and support, the inevitable is experienced with dignity and freedom from pain.

Medicare, Medicaid and most insurance plans pay for hospice services.

When to Consider Hospice Care:

- When your loved one has been diagnosed with a terminal illness and is at the last stages of life.

- When physical, emotional, and spiritual pain and discomfort have progressed and seem unmanageable.

Questions to Ask When Considering Hospice Care:

1. What types of services and support are offered to the patient medically? Emotionally? Spiritually?

2. What types of services/support are offered to the family and caregiver?

3. Will they provide medical equipment, supplies, and respite services?

4. Do they consult with physicians, dieticians, therapists, and pharmacists?

5. Do they provide volunteer services to sit with the patient? If so, are these volunteers medically trained?

6. Is there any bereavement counseling available following the death of the patient?

7. How is the insurance portion handled? Do they accept Medicare, Medicaid, or private insurance?

Where to Find Hospice Care:

• Your hospital discharge planner, social worker, case manager, or a family physician.

• Check with a home health care company for referrals.

• Ask a church or synagogue for referrals.

CHAPTER 4

PRESCRIPTION SAVINGS
FOR SENIORS

Many people, nationwide, of all ages, can't afford their prescription medications. There are resources available to help many of those individuals get prescriptions for free or at considerable discounts, usually directly from pharmaceutical company-sponsored programs.

Partnership for Prescription Assistance Program

The Partnership for Prescription Assistance Program has brought together many of America's pharmaceutical companies and other health care providers, patient advocacy organizations, and community groups to help patients who qualify under certain parameters get their medications for free or at discounted prices. You can contact them at 1-888-477-2669 or www.pparx.org.

In many cases, the qualifications are that the patient must earn less than 200% of the federal poverty level which is considered to be approximately $19,000 for an individual or $32,000 for a family of three.

In 2003, more than 20 million people in the United States made less than the 200% of the federal poverty level and had no health insurance coverage. Currently, individuals 65–69 have an average of 14 prescriptions written per year. Those who are age 80–84 have an average of 18. By 2010, an estimated 80% of healthcare spending will be devoted to the chronically ill. By the year 2030 there will be 70 million people over the age of 65, many with health challenges and needing assistance.

Partnership for Prescription Assistance directs patients to the program that most meets their needs, offering over 2,500 medicines from various companies. The program gathers all of the information needed to see if you qualify and will then create an application that you can print out.

Each patient assistance program has its own criteria for approval. Once you complete the step-by-step application, you should be able to see if you are eligible for one or more of the programs.

Many programs provide prescription assistance for Medicare beneficiaries who do not have full prescription drug benefits. People who enrolled in other public and privately sponsored programs that include prescription drug coverage may not be eligible for assistance; however, there are some instances in which Medicaid beneficiaries may be eligible for certain patient assistance programs.

Although you may already have coverage, you may still qualify for additional assistance. You can even qualify for multiple patient assistance programs if you have a Medicare-approved drug discount card.

The eligibility criteria for patient assistance programs vary from program to program and may even vary by medicines within a particular program, depending on several factors related to income, prescription medicines, resident state, age, and current prescription drug coverage.

The types of information needed to apply include:

- Age.

- State of residence and zip code.

- Estimated gross annual household income.

- Number of people living in household.

- Brand name of prescription medicines currently taken or prescribed.

- Type of health insurance and/or prescription coverage.

Doctors will be responsible for signing patient application forms, adding prescription information, and, depending on the program, possibly mailing or faxing the application on behalf of the patient.

Depending on the program, the medicines are either sent to the doctor's office or sent to the patient's home. Some programs send a pharmacy card in the mail that patients can use to get their free or nearly free medicines at their local pharmacy.

Each program has its own enrollment and renewal requirements. Many of the programs require patients to reapply periodically. The specifics are included in the packet sent to the patient in the mail.

You can also learn about discount programs through these Web sites:

- www.medicare.gov.

- www.helping patients.org.

- www.benefitscheckuprx.com.

- www.togetherrxaccess.com.

- Department of Veteran's Affairs, www.va.gov.

- www.freemedicinefoundation.com.

Medicare

Medicare, the nation's largest health insurance program, currently covers approximately 40 million Americans. The program provides health insurance to people age 65 and over, those who have permanent kidney failure, and certain individuals under 65 with disabilities. Medicare is divided into four parts:

PART A

A component of Medicare fee-for-service that covers:

- in-patient hospital services

- skilled nursing facility services

- certain home health services

- hospice care

PART B

A component of Medicare fee-for-service that covers:

- doctor services

- out-patient hospital services

- certain home health services

- medical equipment and supplies

- laboratory tests

- other health services and supplies

PART C

This is the managed care side of Medicare that is now called the Medicare Advantage Program. It was formerly called Medicare+Choice. It permits Medicare beneficiaries to select health plans in which they can go to doctors, specialists, or hospitals that participate in the plan.

PART D

This part was recently created under the Medicare Prescription Drug, Improvement, and Modernization Act of 2003 (MMA). It provides coverage, which began in 2006, for out-patient prescription drugs.

For more information, one of the easier websites to navigate is located at www. aarpmedicarerx.com. You may call 1-800-495-9137 for AARP Health Options or the national Medicare office at 1-800-633-4227 (1-800-MEDICARE).

Medicaid

Medicaid was created as a jointly-funded program in which the federal government matches state spending to provide medical and health-related services.

The Medicaid program serves:

- Low-income families with children.

- Individuals age 65 and over.

- Blind or disabled persons who are on supplemental security income.

- Certain low-income pregnant women and children.

- Certain low-income people who have very high medical bills.

Under specific qualifying conditions, Medicaid will pay for care in Skilled Nursing Facilities (SNFs) and also Intermediate Care Facilities (ICFs). Depending on the situation, if a person is eligible for both Medicare and Medicaid, Medicare will pay for its allowable benefits timeframe, if all requirements are met, and then Medicaid takes over the financial assistance.

Private Insurance Policies

Some insurance companies offer private insurance policies for long-term nursing home care. These policies vary widely in coverage and cost. Make sure you understand exactly what kind of policy you are purchasing.

Be sure the policy does not duplicate skilled nursing facility coverage provided by any additional care plan, such as Medicare or Medicaid or any other supplemental insurance. Ask about any stipulations that are required before the company will pay benefits. The company may require that a patient have previous hospitalization before benefits are paid out. Some disease conditions such as Alzheimer's and degenerative arthritis do not require hospitalization before nursing care is needed.

Many insurance policies that are purchased prior to skilled nursing care require a waiting period after entrance into a nursing home. It is highly unlikely that nursing care insurance can be purchased after someone enters a facility.

Medigap supplemental insurance is designed to close the gap between medical costs and amounts paid by Medicare. However, both Medicare and Medigap are for short-term use or acute care, not for long-term nursing care.

Specific questions about policies should be directed to your state's insurance commissioner.

CHAPTER 5

REVERSE MORTGAGES

Many seniors spend most of their lives paying for their homes. In 1989, the Federal Housing Authority (FHA) established a Home Equity Conversion Mortgage. Several years later, Fannie Mae set up a conventional reverse mortgage called the Home Keeper Reverse Mortgage.

FHA and Fannie Mae require a free financial counseling session with an impartial, nonprofit agency in order to get approval. Here facts about reverse mortgages:

- The minimum age for applicants is 62, and the home must be a primary residence.

- There are no monthly payments as long as the borrower lives in the home. If they move, or are deceased, the loan becomes due and is generally paid from the proceeds of the sale of the house.

- The loan can be in a lump sum, monthly payments, an equity line of credit, or a combination.

- The money is considered a loan. It is not income and is tax-free.

- Proceeds from the loan should not affect Social Security or Medicare Benefits.

- The loan should not affect Medicaid eligibility or public assistance programs so long as the case does not exceed the limit set by that particular program.

- The loan is due and payable when the last remaining borrower no longer lives in the house as a primary residence. The balance includes the amount used, closing costs and interest accrued on the outstanding balance. The repayment is generally made from the proceeds of the sale of the home.

Keep in mind that these loans are designed to benefit the lender as well, and the borrower should seek legal advice when considering a reverse mortgage.

Further Organizational Help

AAA Foundation for Traffic Safety

607 14th St. NW, Suite 201
Washington, D.C. 20005
1-800-305-7233
www.aaafoundation.org or www.seniordrivers.org

This foundation provides literature and videos on safe driving. There are pamphlets containing self-exams to test driving skills for senior citizens, and training programs are available in specific areas.

AARP

601 E. St. NW
Washington, D.C. 20049
1-888-687-2277
www.aarp.org

AARP has information on a range of age-related topics including housing, home care, volunteer services, stress in caring for aging parents, and an array of insurance and financial subjects. They also provide information on pharmaceutical discount programs, travel, driver safety courses, tax preparation help, financial planning, consumer protection, and health issues.

Administration on Aging

www.aoa.gov/eldfam/eldfam.asp

The AOA website can link you to various websites for medical information on topics such as Alzheimer's disease, arthritis, and diabetes. Other topics include: elder law, mental health, prescription drugs, and financial information, including reverse mortgages, long-term care insurance and elder care costs.

Centers for Medicare & Medicaid Services

7500 Security Blvd.
Baltimore, MD 21244
1-877-267-2323
www.cms.hhs.gov

This website will give you up-to-date information on Medicare and Medicaid and all the services they provide.

Dept. of Veteran's Affairs

1-800-827-1000
www.va.gov

This gives general information and will direct you to specific resources for veterans, including benefits, eligibility, referral sources, and VA medical centers.

Eldercare Locator

800-677-1666
www.eldercare.gov

This is a starting point to guide you to various local resources in your area of interest. It provides articles on eldercare and long-term care, including legal, financial, medical, and housing issues.

National Association of Professional Geriatric Care Managers

1604 N. Country Club Rd.
Tucson, AZ 85716
520-881-8008
www.caremanagers.org

This membership organization provides educational and resource information to caregivers and professionals and an online directory of professional geriatric care managers, listed by state.

National Meals on Wheels Association of America

1414 Prince St., Suite 302
Alexandria, VA 22314
1-703-548-5558
www.mowaa.org

You will be referred to local meal-delivery programs and group dining programs. Frozen meals can also be ordered.

Partnership for Prescription Assistance

1-888-477-2669
www.pparx.org

This is a prescription savings program for eligible individuals who lack prescription drug coverage.

Foundations, Organizations and Associations

There are many wonderful organizations and foundations throughout the country that are available to assist and direct individuals with questions or concerns. The organizations listed below are a small sample that may assist in providing in-depth information for your use.

Alzheimer's Association, 1-800-272-3900, www.alz.org.

Arthritis Foundation, 1-800-283-7800, www.arthritis.org.

American Council of the Blind, 1-800-424-8666, www.acb.org.

American Cancer Society, 1-800-227-2345, www.cancer.org.

American Diabetes Association, 1-800-342-2383, www.diabetes.org.

American Heart Association, 1-800-242-8721, www.americanheart.org.

National Kidney Foundation—1-800-622-9010/www.kidney.org

American Lung Association, 1-800-586-4872, www.lungusa.org.

National Multiple Sclerosis Society, 1-800-344-4867, www.nationalmssociety.org.

American Parkinson Disease Association, 1-800-223-2732, www.apdaparkinson.org.

Chapter 6

Wills, Living Wills, Power of Attorney and Guardianship

By planning ahead and communicating decisions with your loved ones, conflicts and difficulties will be lessened. There will be fewer issues if your loved ones have a will and a living will and establish durable and medical power of attorney for a responsible relative.

Wills

A will is a legal document that directs how your money and other property will be distributed after you die. If you do not have a will, the state will determine who inherits your property upon your death. How you want your property distributed may be very different from the way the state determines distribution. Furthermore, state law may dictate the executor of your estate, your doctors, and other medical providers if you cannot make the decision or if you do not have clearly defined written procedures for doing so. Consulting with a professional estate planner in advance can affect how someone ends up paying for nursing home care. This must be signed, witnessed, and notarized as required by law.

Living Wills

A living will is defined as a document that describes and explains the treatment people want and need when they are not mentally able to make important decisions for themselves. It sets forth their wishes regarding medical intervention if they are in a coma, a persistent vegetative state, or are terminally ill with no reasonable expectation to live without the use of life support.

Medical Power of Attorney

Medical power of attorney allows you to authorize others to make health care decisions for you should you become unable to do so. It does not take the place of your making your own health care decisions should you be able to do so. This is determined by your physicians.

To create medical power of attorney, you sign a paper that says that you want a certain person(s) to make health care decisions for you if you are unable to make those decisions yourself.

Those you choose can then decide on a range of health care issues. This can include whether to admit or discharge you from the hospital or nursing home, what treatments may or may not be given, who can have access to your medical records, how your body is disposed of after death, and decisions regarding an autopsy or funeral arrangements.

A medical power of attorney will tell your agent in writing specifically what it is that you want or don't want. For example, you can direct that you do or do not want to be hooked up to machines that keep you alive or that you do or do not want to be hooked up to feeding tubes that provide food and water. Discuss this with an attorney and or estate planner in order to cover all areas of concern.

Durable Power of Attorney

A durable power of attorney authorizes a person to take care of your financial or business affairs. You can give another person(s) all of your authority or some authority to act on your behalf. Be sure to file notarized copies with appropriate authorities, including care facilities, doctors, attorneys, and accountants or financial advisors.

You can allow your agent to handle all of your financial affairs, including the power to sell, rent, or mortgage your home, pay your bills, cash or deposit checks, buy and sell your stock, investments, or personal items, or you can allow your agent to handle only certain financial affairs such as paying your monthly bills.

If your agent is not following your instructions, you can and should cancel or revoke the document and end your agent's power to act for you.

Guardianship

A guardian is a person appointed by probate court to make decisions for an adult who has been found by the court to be incapacitated and unable to communicate decisions about his or her personal health and safety. Many times, the individual does not have a family member or friend who is able to serve as guardian. In this case, the court may appoint a public guardian who will respect the rights of the incapacitated person.

Some of the things the specially-trained guardian will oversee are:

- Basic daily personal needs such as food, clothing, shelter, medical treatment, and any additional services to provide for the safety and well-being of the individual.

- Filing of any paperwork such as making sure that bills are paid.

- Visitation of the individual on a regular basis.

- Protection of the individual's rights and advocacy for that person.

The primary goal is to enable the ward to retain as much control over his or her life as possible. Limited guardianship is considered when necessary.

Conclusion

Millions of people are actively caring for aging family members or friends. Many are taking on the financial responsibility, in addition to caring for their children and other family members, while having jobs and responsibilities inside and outside of the home.

Just when you think life should be getting a little simpler, you find yourself being pulled into even more directions.

When my own mother went through surgeries and illness, I did everything I could to make the time we spent together as upbeat and positive as possible. There were many times when I was exhausted and stressed, yet I made sure I carved out time to exercise each day. For me, exercising gave me a renewed energy to deal with the issues at hand. During my mother's recovery processes, I took her to my health club, and while I exercised, she watched television, chatted with people, and knitted more scarves than we could count. She knows how important exercise is to my health and well-being. Even now, with her being active and healthy, we both make sure our time together is fun and memorable.

To create the best possible scenario and to lessen the load, use these steps as guidelines:

- Set boundaries—Care taking functions and responsibilities can change dramatically. We must strive to maintain respect for each other as we negotiate and agonize over life-changing decisions together.

- Talk openly about concerns—Through thoughtful communication, we can ease the guilt and stress we are feeling about this new dynamic. It is important to differentiate between serious health risks and honest differences of opinion. Be sensitive to the elderly person's desire to hold on to independence. Continuously remind them that you are there to work with them, not against them.

- Find ways to communicate when you are together—Try to get your loved one to talk about wonderful moments from the past. You may find out things you didn't know. Just being together and participating in activities can give everyone new memories to cherish. Go to a grandchild's school event, a movie, lunch, or bookstore. Visit the zoo, an art exhibit, aquarium or sporting event.

- Consider financial plans and arrangements—Meeting with legal and financial authorities will ensure a smoother transition when decisions need to be made.

- Take advantage of enlisting help from others at all possible opportunities—Ask for help from family, friends, clergy members, physicians, and volunteer organizations. Many companies provide assistance through an employee benefits program or human resources. A team effort from family and friends will help reduce feelings of guilt and anxiety. We are much more effective when we are surrounded by a strong support group.

- Maintain relationships with others—We need to find a delicate balance between caring for ourselves and caring for others. Get adequate sleep, exercise, eat healthy foods, and set aside some time, no matter how brief, to have fun and laugh.

- Seek professional help when necessary—When we feel overwhelmed with family responsibilities, caring for an elderly person, and working, often times, talking with medical professionals, clergy members, friends, family members, or caregiver support groups can help tremendously. The simple act of keeping a journal of our feelings and getting them on paper can make us feel better.

- Know that there are many options available—When loved ones resist needed changes, ease them into a situation and make them part of the decision-making process. This is about striking a balance in their health, safety, and well-being. Exploring opportunities together can show them that you are trying to help them maintain as much independence as possible.

- Check in with yourself on a regular basis to make sure you are getting the help you need and taking care of yourself—and do not feel guilty about it—this benefits those you take care of too!

More than likely, this will be a very intense time for everyone involved. Your loved one may respond with feelings of depression, anger, resentment, or regression. If this happens, it may cause you to be angry, depressed, or frustrated. These are natural reactions to the dramatic changes that are taking place. Most often, they will pass.

Always remember that you are doing the best that you can in uncharted territory. We are all human and make mistakes that we can learn from. Regardless of the severity of the situation, don't forget to nurture yourself. Find the frequency and balance necessary that works for you. When we respect our limits, we make things better for our loved ones. Neglecting other responsibilities and exhausting ourselves to constantly be by their side isn't healthy for anyone.

And, take heart, entering a care facility does not have to be the end of the road. Your loved ones may be able to build friendships and have worthwhile experiences in their new home. It is possible for us all to create positive memories and loving relationships during this stressful time.

ABOUT THE AUTHOR

Hillary Abrams lives in Atlanta, Georgia. She graduated from the University of Georgia with degrees in journalism and psychology. She began her career in healthcare in the early 1990s with emphasis on the aging population. She currently consults with families, professionals, and employees of organizations concerning levels of care and assistance for the elderly.

NOTES:

Notes:

NOTES:

NOTES:

Notes:

NOTES:

LaVergne, TN USA
26 March 2010
177314LV00003B/16/P